"What does it mean to take up your cross and follow Jesus Christ? How can you be heavenly minded and yet do much earthly good? Calvin addresses these practical questions and more in this excerpt from his classic, *Institutes of the Christian Religion*. I love this little book, and heartily endorse this judiciously translated and edited printing that makes Calvin even more accessible to the modern reader."

—DR. JOEL R. BEEKE
PRESIDENT, PURITAN REFORMED THEOLOGICAL SEMINARY
GRAND RAPIDS, MICH.

"We are living in a golden age of Christian publishing. Readers are being served with new works written here in the twenty-first century and, perhaps even more importantly, with classics from days gone by. This booklet is one of those classics, and I'm grateful to Aaron Denlinger and Burk Parsons for allowing today's Christians to rediscover it. I pray that it blesses us just as it blessed many of our forebears."

—TIM CHALLIES
BLOGGER AT CHALLIES.COM
TORONTO

"I have often thought, 'I would love to retranslate for the twenty-first century the life-shaping material in Calvin's *Institutes* book 3, chapters 6–10,' and I've done nothing! But now, Burk Parsons and Aaron Denlinger have done the job for us all. We owe them a big thank you, because every Christian needs to have a working knowledge of this little book."

—DR. SINCLAIR B. FERGUSON
TEACHING FELLOW, LIGONIER MINISTRIES

"The smooth and pleasant Latin Calvin wrote has found a just as smooth and pleasant translation in this wonderful little book. That sure is an accomplishment and will help many to enjoy even more the timeless message this treasure contains."

—DR. HERMAN J. SELDERHUIS
PROFESSOR OF CHURCH HISTORY,
THEOLOGICAL UNIVERSITY APELDOORN
APELDOORN, THE NETHERLANDS

"Calvin's treatment of the Christian life in book 3 of his *Institutes* is a treasure. For more than five hundred years, Christian believers have profited from the clear way in which Calvin describes the Christian life of self-denial and cross-bearing in union with Jesus Christ. Reformation Trust Publishing's fresh translation of this Christian classic is a most welcome addition to earlier publications of Calvin's masterful description of life in conformity to Christ."

—DR. CORNELIS P. VENEMA
PRESIDENT AND PROFESSOR OF DOCTRINAL STUDIES,
MID-AMERICA REFORMED SEMINARY
DYER, IND.

JOHN CALVIN

A LITTLE BOOK

ON THE

CHRISTIAN
LIFE

JOHN CALVIN

A LITTLE BOOK
ON THE
CHRISTIAN
LIFE

TRANSLATED AND EDITED BY

AARON CLAY DENLINGER
AND BURK PARSONS

 Ligonier Ministries

A Little Book on the Christian Life
© 2017 by Aaron Clay Denlinger and Burk Parsons

Published by Ligonier Ministries
421 Ligonier Court, Sanford, FL 32771
Ligonier.org

Printed in China
Amity Printing Company
0000923
First edition, twelfth printing

ISBN 978-1-56769-744-5 (Paperback)
ISBN 978-1-56769-745-2 (ePub)
ISBN 978-1-56769-746-9 (Kindle)

Cover and interior design: Metaleap Creative metaleapcreative.com
Interior design and typeset: Katherine Lloyd, The DESK
Prisse d'Avennes, Emile (1807-79) / Private Collection / The Stapleton Collection / Bridgeman Images

Scripture quotations are from the ESV® Bible (The Holy Bible, English Standard Version®), copyright © 2001 by Crossway, a publishing ministry of Good News Publishers. Used by permission. All rights reserved.

The Library of Congress has cataloged the Reformation Trust edition as follows:

Names: Calvin, Jean, 1509-1564, author. | Denlinger, Aaron C. (Aaron Clay), editor, translator. | Parsons, Burk, editor, translator.
Title: A little book on the Christian life / John Calvin ; edited and translated by Aaron Clay Denlinger and Burk Parsons.
Other titles: De vita hominis Christiani. English
Description: Orlando, FL : Reformation Trust Publishing, A Division of Ligonier Ministries, 2017. | Includes bibliographical references and index.
Identifiers: LCCN 2016044699 | ISBN 9781567697445
Subjects: LCSH: Christian life.
Classification: LCC BV4501.3 .C355313 2017 | DDC 248.4/842—dc23
LC record available at https://lccn.loc.gov/2016044699

I offer my heart to you,
O Lord, promptly and sincerely.

JOHN CALVIN (1509–1564)

TABLE OF CONTENTS

PREFACE

THE TEACHING ON the Christian life in this book is extracted from John Calvin's most famous theological work, the *Institutes of the Christian Religion*. Calvin's *Institutes* underwent multiple editions during his own lifetime, with each one incorporating substantial addition to the work. The first edition of the work appeared in 1536, roughly one year after Calvin's flight from France for the safer haven of the Swiss town of Basel. Calvin was twenty-seven years old with merely several years of self-study in theology under his belt when the *Institutes* first appeared, a fact often rehearsed to demoralize middle-aged, aspiring theologians or browbeat younger ones into greater productivity. Yet the first edition of the *Institutes* was only a bare outline of what the work would become as it was tweaked and increased by the Reformer over the next two decades. That first edition contained only six chapters covering the basics of the Christian faith, in contrast to the eighty chapters divided into four books that would constitute the final Latin edition of Calvin's work in 1559.

The first edition of the *Institutes* promised in its full title a "complete summary of piety" in addition to "whatever is necessary to be known in doctrine." To all appearances, the young Reformer soon realized that he had promised more than he had delivered in the work. In 1539, he published a second and substantially expanded edition of the *Institutes* that "now at last," its revised name promised, "truly answered to its title." For our purposes, the most intriguing addition to this second edition was the chapter titled *De vita hominis Christiani* (On the life of a Christian man). This chapter included in relatively mature form all that Calvin would say about the Christian life in subsequent editions—both Latin and French—of the *Institutes*.

The value of this chapter "on the life of a Christian man" as a treatise in its own right, independent of its larger context in the *Institutes*, was quickly realized after the publication of the 1539 *Institutes*. In 1540, a Parisian Huguenot (and future martyr) by the name of Pierre de la Place translated the chapter into French, one year before Calvin completed his first French edition of the entire *Institutes*. De la Place's translation never saw publication, though it circulated widely enough to secure a place on the University of Paris's Index of Prohibited Books several years later. In 1549, an English translation of the chapter by Thomas Broke, a largely unknown English Reformer, was published in London under the title *Of the Life or Conversation of a Christian Man*. This, intriguingly, was more than a decade before a complete English edition of Calvin's *Institutes* appeared in print.[1]

Calvin authorized an independent Latin edition of his work on the Christian life in 1550, the

---

1 More detailed historical information on the publication history of Calvin's work on the Christian life can be found in David Clyde Jones, "The Curious History of John Calvin's Golden Booklet of the Christian Life," *Presbyterion* 35/2 (2009): 82–86. Pierre de la Place's martyrdom is described in John Foxe's *Book of Martyrs* (London: Knight and Son, 1854), 204–6.

same year that a fourth Latin edition of the *Institutes* appeared. The title of that independent Latin treatise, which translates as "A distinguished little book on the life of a Christian man" (*De vita hominis Christiani, insigne opusculum*), was probably decided by the publisher, but is notable because it very likely served as the basis for the much later Dutch and English designations of Calvin's work on the Christian life as the "Golden Booklet."

The 1550 *De vita hominis Christiani, insigne opusculum* was published in Geneva, which Calvin called home from 1541 until his death in 1564. Geneva likewise served as the base for stand-alone publications of Calvin's work on the Christian life in French (*Traicte tresexcellent de la vie Chrestienne*) in 1550 and 1552 and for the publication of his work on the Christian life in Italian (*Breve et utile trattato de la vita de l'huomo christiano*) in 1561, prior—as was the case in English—to the publication of a complete Italian translation of the

Institutes. All subsequent early modern renditions of Calvin's work on the Christian life, no matter the language, would be incorporated into print runs of his entire *Institutes* (of which there were many), with the possible exception of one further English translation and publication of the independent work in 1594.

The mid-nineteenth century, however, would see renewed interest in translating and publishing Calvin's work on the Christian life as an independent treatise. In 1857, a Dutchman named Petrus Georg Bartels published a German translation of Calvin's work on the Christian life titled *Büchlein vom Leben eines Christenmenschen* (Booklet on the life of a Christian man). Successive Dutch translations of Bartels' German rendering of Calvin's work followed in 1858 and 1859 under the title *Johannes Calvijn's gulden boekske, over den regt christelijken wandel* (John Calvin's Golden Booklet concerning right Christian walking).

The twentieth century witnessed multiple Dutch printings and editions of the *Gulden Boekske* (1906, 1938, 1950, and 1983). Given the popularity that Calvin's work on the Christian life came to enjoy as an independent treatise in twentieth-century Dutch Reformed circles, it's unsurprising that it was a Dutchman who produced in 1952 an English version of Calvin's work on the Christian life under the title *Golden Booklet of the True Christian Life*. The Dutchman in question, Henry Van Andel, immigrated to America in 1909, and served as professor of Dutch language, literature, and culture at Calvin College from 1915 to 1950. Van Andel's work, however, was no mere English translation of its Dutch counterparts of similar title. It was, rather, a fresh translation of Calvin's work on the Christian life from the definitive Latin (1559) and French (1560) editions of the *Institutes*. Van Andel's work would eventually see multiple editions, and would itself—rather curiously—be translated from English into multiple other languages.

More recent translations of Calvin's work on the Christian life have been made. In 2002, Elsie Anne McKee, professor of Reformation studies and the history of worship at Princeton Theological Seminary, included substantial extracts from Calvin's work on the Christian life in an anthology of Calvin's writings on pastoral piety. And in 2009, the Banner of Truth Trust produced a new translation of Calvin's work on the Christian life—based on the final French edition of the *Institutes* and completed by Robert White—under the title *A Guide to Christian Living*.

Nevertheless, Van Andel's translation remains the standard edition of Calvin's work on the Christian life as an independent treatise. That fact may seem curious to those who compare Van Andel's translation to Calvin's original work in Latin or French, or even to the relevant chapters in one of the better-known English translations of Calvin's entire *Institutes*. Despite his stated intention, in the preface to his work, of adhering to the original text "as closely as possible," Van Andel took considerable liberties with Calvin's text, both in terms of form and content. With regard to form, Van Andel subdivided Calvin's own paragraphs into discretely numbered sections, often producing, in that process, grammatically awkward paragraphs of merely one or two sentences and, even more problematically, obscuring the flow of Calvin's argument. With regard to context, Van Andel's work too often reads more like a paraphrase of Calvin than a proper translation. Van Andel, by his own testimony, sought to retain Calvin's "meaning," but to render that meaning in "imaginative language." In the end, however, comprehensibility and colorfulness seem to trump faithfulness to Calvin's original in his translation. With all due deference to Van Andel's intention, then, we concur with the late

Calvin scholar T.H.L. Parker who, with reference to Van Andel's work, observed that anyone wishing "to know and understand Calvin on the Christian life will be well advised not to attempt it by way of this edition."[2]

Consequently, we believe the church will be well served by a new translation of Calvin's work on the Christian life—a translation based principally upon the final and definitive Latin edition of Calvin's *Institutes*. Our aim in completing this project has generally been to produce a translation that we believe Calvin himself would have been pleased with. We have, in other words, aimed at faithfulness not just to Calvin's meaning but, so much as possible, to his own words. We have, however, also striven to make Calvin's meaning as clear as possible to English readers. Our efforts in this regard have

2 T.H.L. Parker, "Review of John Calvin, *Golden Booklet of the True Christian Life*, trans. by H.J. Van Andel," in *Evangelical Quarterly* 24 (1952): 185–86.

required us to break some of Calvin's lengthier sentences into shorter ones, to introduce more frequent paragraph breaks than Calvin's work contains, and to replace some pronouns with their stated antecedents to maximize clarity. We have also consistently opted for English equivalents to Latin words and phrases that are familiar to English speakers, even if that at times meant bypassing an obvious English derivative or cognate of a Latin word.

The very close and deliberate reading of Calvin's words on the Christian life that this project required from us was more rewarding than either of us could have anticipated. Translation sessions regularly evolved—or perhaps devolved—into lengthy discussions of discrete points made by Calvin about the realities of Christian living. Amid those discussions, Calvin often seemed to be more of a living conversation partner than the dead and buried author of the text before us. We hope that others, in reading this work, will experience Calvin conversing with them—comforting and exhorting them—as powerfully as we did as we labored on it.

We wish, finally, to express our gratitude to Thomas Brewer for his invaluable editorial insight and assistance in the production of this book. Without his help, this book would not be what it is.

—AARON CLAY DENLINGER AND BURK PARSONS

SCRIPTURE'S CALL

TO CHRISTIAN LIVING

THE GOAL OF God's work in us is to bring our lives into harmony and agreement with His own righteousness, and so to manifest to ourselves and others our identity as His adopted children. We discover in God's law a picture of God's own image, to which we are being progressively conformed. But since we are lazy and require prodding and encouragement in this, it will be helpful to construct in this work a model of the mature Christian life from various passages of Scripture, so that those who are truly repentant of heart will not lose their way on the path to greater conformity to God's image.

I know that in addressing the topic of the mature Christian life, I am entering on a vast and complex subject. Even if I were merely to summarize all that has been written by others on this topic, the result would be a long and dense volume. Previous generations of theologians have written large works on individual virtues, but they wasted no words. For when anyone seeks to describe and commend a particular virtue, it seems as if his pen is spontaneously led to write at great length because of the significance of his subject. Indeed, one will not seem to have described any particular virtue sufficiently unless he writes at great length.

In this work, however, it's not my intention to say too much, nor to discuss every virtue in great detail, nor to stray into lengthy exhortations. Such exhortations can be found in the writings of those who have gone before us, especially in the sermons of the church fathers. My goal here is simply to present to godly people a model for ordering their lives. I intend, that is, to identify a certain universal principle to guide Christians in their duties. Perhaps in the future I will have time to address the subject of Christian virtues more fully. Or maybe others better suited to the task will do so. By nature I love brevity, so perhaps even if I tried to write something larger I would not succeed in my effort. In any case, even if a longer work on the subject of the Christian life were worthwhile, I would hesitate to attempt such now, because my purpose in this work is to present doctrine simply and concisely.

When philosophers write about the virtuous life, they identify certain primary goals for human beings such as integrity and honor, and from these they derive specific duties and the entire chorus of remaining virtues. But Scripture has its own order and plan that is more beautiful and certain than any philosophic method. The philosophers, wanting to draw attention to themselves, strive to be very clear—clear, that is, in showcasing their own rhetorical skills. But the Spirit of God lacks such a motive in His teaching. He has not, therefore, followed the specific method of the philosophers, though he has revealed truth clearly enough to keep us from despising clarity. ♦

THERE ARE TWO main parts to the instruction from Scripture on the Christian life that follow. The first is that a love of righteousness—to which we are not naturally prone—must be implanted and poured into our hearts. The second is that we need some model that will keep us from losing our way in our pursuit of righteousness. Scripture contains many arguments to encourage us on the path of righteousness. Many of these arguments I have noted elsewhere,[1] and some I note here.

To begin with, what better foundation can Scripture give for the pursuit of righteousness than to tell us we should be holy because God Himself is holy? Moreover, when we were scattered and wandering like sheep, lost in the maze of the world, God found us and gathered us to Himself. When we contemplate this relationship between ourselves and God, let us remember that holiness is the bond of our union with Him. Not, of course, because we enter into fellowship

---

1 For example, in Calvin's discussion of the majesty of God (*Institutes* 1.1.2–3) and in his discussion of conversion (*Institutes* 2.3.6).

with Him by the merit of our own holiness. Rather, we first of all cling to Him, and then, having received His holiness, we follow wherever He calls us. For it is characteristic of His glory that He has no fellowship with sin and impurity. Holiness is the goal of our calling. Therefore we must consistently set our sights upon holiness if we would rightly respond to God's calling. To what purpose did God pull us out of the wickedness and pollution of this world—wickedness and pollution in which we were submerged—if we allow ourselves to wallow in such wickedness and pollution for the rest of our lives?

Furthermore, if we count ourselves among God's people, Scripture tells us to live as citizens of the holy city of Jerusalem, which He has consecrated to Himself.

> For here we have no lasting city, but we seek the city that is to come.
>
> HEBREWS 13:14

It's shameful that the citizens of the holy city should pollute it by their impurity. Thus, we read that there will be a dwelling place in God's tabernacle for those who walk blamelessly and pursue righteousness. It's not right that the sanctuary in which God dwells should resemble a filthy stable. ♦

TO PROMPT US toward righteousness more effectively, Scripture tells us that God the Father, who has reconciled us to Himself in His Anointed One, Jesus Christ, has given us in Christ a model to which we should conform our lives. You will not find a better model in the philosophers—in whom many expect to find the only correct and orderly treatment of moral philosophy. They, while doing their best to encourage us to be virtuous, have nothing to say except that we should live "according to nature." Scripture, however, draws its encouragement from the true fountain. It teaches us to contemplate our lives in relation to God, our Author, to whom we are bound. And, having taught us that we have fallen from the true state and condition of our original creation, Scripture adds that Christ, through whom we have been restored to favor with God, is set before us as a model whose form and beauty should be reflected in our own lives. What could be more effective than this? Indeed, what more is needed than this? We have been adopted by the Lord as children with this understanding—that in our lives we should mirror Christ who is the bond of our adoption. And truly, unless we are devoted—even addicted—to righteousness, we will faithlessly abandon our Creator and disown Him as our Savior.

Scripture derives some principle of conduct from every gift of God described to us in it, and from every aspect of our salvation. God has manifested Himself as Father to us. If we do not manifest ourselves as sons to Him in turn, we prove ourselves to be extremely ungrateful (Mal. 1:6; 1 John 3:1).

> Therefore be imitators of God, as beloved children.

EPHESIANS 5:1

Christ has cleansed us by washing us with His blood, and has communicated this cleansing to us through baptism.[2] It would be inappropriate, therefore, for us to defile ourselves with fresh filthiness (1 Cor. 6:11; Eph. 5:26; Heb. 10:10; 1 Peter 1:15, 19). Christ has engrafted us into His body. We, therefore, who are His members must be especially careful not to fling mud or filthiness on the body of Christ (John 15:3–6; 1 Cor. 6:15; Eph. 5:23–33). Christ our Head has ascended into heaven. We, therefore, must set aside earthly affections and wholeheartedly long for that place (Col. 3:1ff.). The Holy Spirit has consecrated us

---

2 Calvin acknowledges baptism as an instrument of the realities it represents, provided the sacrament is accompanied by faith. "But from this sacrament, as from all others, we obtain only as much as we receive by faith" (*Institutes* 4.15.15).

as temples of God. We, therefore, must let the glory of God shine through us, and we must not pollute ourselves with sin. Our bodies and souls have been destined to heavenly incorruption and an unfading crown. We, therefore, must strive upward—keeping ourselves pure and incorruptible until the Day of the Lord (1 Thess. 5:23). These are most holy foundations on which to build the Christian life. Nothing like these can be found in the philosophers, who in their commendation of virtue never rise above the dignity that natural man can achieve. ♦

SOMETHING MUST BE said about those who want to be called Christians but possess nothing of Christ except the title and appearance. They arrogantly glory in His holy name. But only those who have gained a true knowledge of Christ from the Word of the gospel have a relationship with Him. And the Apostle denies that any have rightly learned Christ who have not learned that they must put off the old man, who is corrupted by deceitful desires, and put on Christ.

> But that is not the way you learned Christ!—assuming that you have heard about him and were taught in him, as the truth is in Jesus, to put off your old self, which belongs to your former manner of life and is corrupt through deceitful desires, and to be renewed in the spirit of your minds, and to put on the new self, created after the likeness of God in true righteousness and holiness.
>
> **EPHESIANS 4:20–24**

Such nominal Christians demonstrate their knowledge of Christ to be false and offensive no matter how eloquently and loudly they talk about the gospel. For true doctrine is not a matter of the tongue, but of life; neither is Christian doctrine grasped only by the intellect and memory, as truth is grasped in other fields of study. Rather, doctrine is rightly received when it takes possession of the entire soul and finds a dwelling place and shelter in the most intimate affections of the heart. So let such people stop lying, or let them prove themselves worthy disciples of Christ, their teacher.

We have given priority to doctrine, which contains our religion, since it establishes our salvation. But in order for doctrine to be fruitful to us, it must overflow into our hearts, spread into our daily routines, and truly transform us within. Even the philosophers rage against and reject those who profess an art that ought to govern one's life, but who twist that art hypocritically into empty chatter. How much more then should we detest the foolish talk of those who give lip service to the gospel? The gospel's power ought to penetrate the innermost affections of the heart, sink down into the soul, and inspire the whole man a hundred times more than the lifeless teachings of the philosophers. ♦

I'M NOT SAYING that the conduct of a Christian will breathe nothing but pure gospel, although this should be desired and pursued. I'm not, in other words, talking about gospel perfection, as if I were unwilling to acknowledge or recognize a man or a woman as a Christian who has not obtained perfection. If that were the case, everyone would be excluded from the church, since we do not find any in it who are close to being perfect. Indeed, we find many in the church who have progressed little toward perfection, but who, nevertheless, it would be unjust to reject as Christians.

What I am saying is this: Let us fix our eyes on the goal and sole object of our pursuit. Let that goal, toward which we must strive and contend, be established from the beginning. After all, it's not right to barter with God regarding what we will and won't undertake from those things He has prescribed for us in His Word. God always commends—as of utmost importance—integrity[3] as the principal part of His worship.

> And as for you, if you will walk before me, as David your father walked, with integrity of heart and uprightness, doing according to all that I have commanded you, and keeping my statutes and my rules, then I will establish your royal throne over Israel forever, as I promised David your father, saying, "You shall not lack a man on the throne of Israel."
>
> 1 KINGS 9:4–5

And by the word *integrity* He means sincere simplicity of heart, free from pretense and deceit, which is the

---

3　See Genesis 17:1–2; 1 Kings 9:4–5; Psalm 41:12.

opposite of duplicity of heart. In other words, right living has a spiritual basis where the inner affection of the soul is sincerely devoted to God for the nurture of holiness and righteousness.

Of course, none of us is capable of running swiftly on the right course while we remain in the earthly confinement of our bodies. Indeed, most of us are so oppressed with weakness that we make little progress—staggering, limping, and crawling on the ground. But let us move forward according to the measure of our resources and pursue the path we have begun to walk. None of us will move forward with so little success that we will not make some daily progress in the way. Therefore, let us keep trying so that we might continually make some gains in the way of the Lord, and neither let us despair over how small our successes are. For however much our successes fall short of our desire, our efforts aren't in vain when we are farther along today than yesterday. So let us fix our eyes on the goal with sincerity and simplicity, aspiring to that end—neither foolishly congratulating ourselves, nor excusing our evil deeds. Let us press on with continual striving toward that goal so that we might surpass ourselves—until we have finally arrived at perfection itself. This, indeed, is what we follow after and pursue all our lives, but we will only possess it when we have escaped the weakness of the flesh and have been received into His perfect fellowship.

SELF-DENIAL IN

THE CHRISTIAN LIFE

THE LAW OF the Lord is the best and most suitable instruction for the proper ordering of our lives. Nevertheless, it seemed good to our heavenly teacher to conform us by an even more precise rule than what's given in the precepts of the law. This is the sum of that rule: It is the duty of believers to present their bodies as living sacrifices, holy and acceptable to God. And in this consists genuine worship of Him. From this rule is derived the exhortation that believers not be conformed to this world, but be transformed by the renewal of their minds, so that by testing they may discern what is the will of God.

> I appeal to you therefore, brothers, by the mercies of God, to present your bodies as a living sacrifice, holy and acceptable to God, which is your spiritual worship. Do not be conformed to this world, but be transformed by the renewal of your mind, that by testing you may

discern what is the will of God, what is good and acceptable and perfect.

ROMANS 12:1–2

This is a marvelous thing—we are consecrated and dedicated to God to the end that we might not think, speak, meditate, or act unless it be to His glory. The sacred can't be put to profane use without injustice to God.

If we are not our own but the Lord's, it's clear what errors we must flee, and what we must direct our whole lives toward. We are not our own; therefore, neither our reason nor our will should dominate our plans and actions. We are not our own; therefore, let us not make the gratification of our flesh our end. We are not our own; therefore, as much as possible, let us forget ourselves and our own interests.

Rather, we are God's. Therefore, let us live and die to Him. We are God's. Therefore, let His wisdom and His will govern all our actions. We are God's. Therefore, let us—in every way in all our lives—run to Him as our only proper end. How far has he progressed who's been taught that he is not his own—who's taken rule and dominion away from his own reason and entrusted them to God. For the plague of submitting to our own rule leads us straight to ruin, but the surest way to safety is neither to know nor to want anything on our own, but simply to follow the leading of the Lord.

Let then our first step be to abandon ourselves, that we may apply all our strength to obedience to God. When I say "obedience," I don't mean giving lip service to God; but rather, being free from the desire of the flesh, turning our minds over completely to the bidding of the Spirit of God. The philosophers are ignorant of this transformation (which Paul calls the "renewing of the mind") even though it constitutes the very beginning of life

(Eph. 4:23). They enthrone man's reason alone as ruler, and they think it alone should be listened to. Indeed, they grant and entrust government of conduct to human reason alone. But Christian philosophy, on the other hand, orders human reason to give place—to submit and yield—to the Holy Spirit. For it's not now we who live, but Christ who lives and reigns in us (Gal. 2:20). ♦

ANOTHER POINT FOLLOWS: We shouldn't seek our own interests but those that are the Lord's, and we should work to promote His glory. This is great progress in the Christian life—that we nearly forget ourselves, that in all matters we hold our own concerns in less esteem, and that we faithfully strive to devote our energies to God and His commands. For when Scripture orders us to disregard our own concerns, it eradicates from our souls the desire to possess things for ourselves, to love power, and to long for the praise of men. Moreover, it uproots our appetite for ambition as well as our appetite for all human glory and other more secret evils. It's indeed fitting that the Christian consider that his entire life stands in relation to God. Just as he submits all he is and does to God's judgment and decision, so also he religiously refers every intention of his mind to God. For the one who has learned to regard God in everything he does is at the same time being drawn away from every vain thought.

This is the self-denial that Christ diligently commended to His disciples from the very beginning of their apprenticeship.

> Then Jesus told his disciples, "If anyone would come after me, let him deny himself and take up his cross and follow me."
>
> **MATTHEW 16:24**

Once self-denial has occupied the heart, it crowds out the evils of pride, arrogance, and pretentiousness as well as greed, lust, gluttony, cowardice, and everything else that is born of self-love. On the other hand, where self-denial does not reign, the worst vices thrive shamelessly. Or, if there is any semblance of virtue, it's corrupted by a depraved desire for glory. No man wants to freely do what is right without first renouncing himself according to God's command. Those who haven't been overcome by this sense of need for self-denial have followed virtue for the sake of praise. Moreover, many philosophers, being overcome with arrogance, have recommended seeking virtue for its own sake. They recommend seeking virtue only for the sake of pride. Yet God isn't pleased with those who strive after fleeting praise. He isn't pleased with those who have puffed-up hearts and who manifest to others that they have received their reward in this life (Matt. 6:5–6, 16). Prostitutes and tax collectors are nearer to the kingdom of heaven than such people.

Jesus said to them, "Truly, I say to you, the tax collectors and the prostitutes go into the kingdom of God before you. For John came to you in the way of righteousness, and you did not believe him, but the tax collectors and the prostitutes believed him. And even when you saw it, you did not afterward change your minds and believe him."

MATTHEW 21:31–32

Nevertheless, we still need to understand clearly the nature of the obstacles that hinder a man, when he does not deny himself, from walking the right path. For rightly it has been said, "There is a world of vices hidden in the soul of man." You won't find any proper remedy to such vices other than to deny yourself, to disregard your own ambitions, and to stretch your mind to seek wholly those things that the Lord requires of you—and to seek them because they are pleasing to Him. ♦

IN ANOTHER PLACE in Scripture, Paul more clearly—albeit briefly—rehearses the various parts of the well-ordered life. "For the grace of God has appeared, bringing salvation for all people, training us to renounce ungodliness and worldly passions, and to live self-controlled, upright, and godly lives in the present age, waiting for our blessed hope, the appearing of the glory of our great God and Savior Jesus Christ, who gave himself for us to redeem us from all lawlessness and to purify for himself a people for his own possession who are zealous for good works" (Titus 2:11–14). In this passage, after Paul sets forth the grace of God to motivate us, he removes two obstacles that severely hinder us in order to clear our path to worship God: first, our natural inclination toward ungodliness; and second, worldly desires that seek to ensnare us all the more. By "ungodliness" he means not only superstition, but anything that contends seriously with the fear of God. By "worldly desires" he means the desires of the flesh. Thus, he orders us, making reference to each table of the law,[1] to put off our natural inclinations and to deny ourselves—that is, to resist whatever our reason and will demand.

Now, every right action in life belongs to one of three categories: self-control, uprightness, and godliness. Of these, self-control means purity and self-restraint, as well as blamelessly and carefully using the things we have, and acting with patience when we lack anything. Uprightness means observing all the requirements of justice so that we render to each one what is rightly due him. Godliness separates us from the impurities of the world and unites us to God in genuine holiness. These three—self-control, uprightness, and godliness—when they are joined together in an unbreakable bond, make us complete. But in truth, nothing is more difficult than saying goodbye to carnal reason and

---

1 The Ten Commandments were given on two tablets ("tables") of stone. These two tablets correspond to God's commands regarding Himself and God's commands regarding our neighbor.

subduing—indeed, conquering—our desires and joining ourselves to God and our brothers. We are, essentially, contemplating the life of the angels even as we trudge through the mire of earth's filthiness. Paul recalls us to the hope of blessed immortality in order to free our souls from all snares, and he admonishes us not to contend for such righteousness without hope. For Christ has first appeared as our Redeemer, and, by His second coming, He will bring forth the fruit of the redemption He has secured for us. In this way, Paul subdues all the temptations that vex us and that keep us from aspiring to heavenly glory. Indeed, he teaches us to live as strangers in this world so that we won't lose our heavenly inheritance. ♦

MOREOVER, WE UNDERSTAND from this passage, Titus 2:11–14, that the denial of ourselves is partly in reference to men and is partly—indeed, chiefly—in reference to God. Scripture orders us to live with men in such a way as to prefer their honor to our own and to devote ourselves in good faith to promoting their welfare (Rom. 12:10).

> Do nothing from selfish ambition or conceit, but in humility count others more significant than yourselves.
>
> PHILIPPIANS 2:3

Thus it gives us commands that our souls are incapable of fulfilling unless our souls are emptied of their natural inclination. Each of us thinks we have just cause for elevating ourselves and despising all others in comparison to ourselves—our self-love ruins us with such blindness. If, in fact, God has gifted us with something that is good in itself, we immediately make it the basis for praising ourselves to such a degree that we not only swell up but almost burst with pride.

We carefully conceal our abundant vices from others—and we pretend they're small and insignificant. In fact, we so delude ourselves that we sometimes embrace our vices as virtues. When others possess gifts that we would admire in ourselves—or even better gifts—we spitefully ridicule and degrade their gifts, refusing to rightly acknowledge them as gifts. Similarly, when others possess vices, we're not content merely to point them out and harshly and sternly reproach them, but we wickedly exaggerate them. Thus our arrogance grows as we seek to exalt ourselves above others, as if we were different from them. Truly, there's no one who does not flippantly and boldly disregard and despise others as inferiors. Yes, the poor outwardly defer to the rich, common people to nobles, servants to masters, the unlearned to the educated. But there's not one who does not nourish a high opinion of himself within.

Everyone flatters himself and carries, as it were, a kingdom in his breast. Consider arrogant men who, in order to gratify themselves, criticize the character and morals of others. And when contention arises, their venom erupts. As long as everything is going smoothly and pleasantly, they present themselves with a kind of gentleness. But in reality, how few there are who can maintain such a superficial appearance of modesty when they are jabbed and aggravated. The only remedy for this is to uproot these toxic diseases—love of strife and love of self—that are implanted deeply within us. Scripture does this uprooting with its teaching. For it teaches us that those things that God has given us are not in any way goods originating from ourselves. Instead, they are free gifts from God.

> Every good gift and every perfect gift
> is from above, coming down from the
> Father of lights with whom there is no
> variation or shadow due to change.
>
> JAMES 1:17

Those who brag about the gifts they have show themselves to be ungrateful. "For who sees anything different in you?" as Paul says. "What do you have that you did not receive? If then you received it, why do you boast as if you did not receive it?" (1 Cor. 4:7). By constant recognition of our vices, let us return to humility. By so doing, there will be nothing left in us to puff us up, but, on the contrary, there will be much to put us in our place.

On the other hand, we are called to respect and commend whatever gifts of God we see in others, and to honor those in whom such gifts reside. For it would be shameful for us to withhold honor from those whom God has deemed worthy of honor. Moreover, so as not to insult those to whom we owe honor and goodwill, we are taught to overlook their vices—though not, of course, to encourage their vices by admiring them. In this way, we will act not only with moderation and modesty, but with grace and friendliness toward others. We will never achieve genuine meekness except by having our hearts saturated with self-denial and respect for others. ♦

WE WILL MEET many difficulties as we try to dutifully seek the good of our neighbors. We won't make any headway in this regard unless we lay aside concern for ourselves—indeed, unless we somehow lay aside our very self. For how, unless we forsake ourselves and commit ourselves wholly to others, can we bring forth those works that Paul identifies as love? "Love," he says, "is patient and kind; love does not envy or boast; it is not arrogant or rude. It does not insist on its own way; it is not irritable;"[2] and so on. That single command that we not insist on our own way—with what force must we resist our own nature to pursue it. Our very nature inclines us toward self-love. As a result, we don't easily deny ourselves or our desires in order to seek the good of others. Even less are we

---

2 1 Corinthians 13:4–5.

willing to give up our right to something and give that right to another.

In order to lead us by the hand to such self-denial, Scripture warns us that whatever we have freely received from the Lord is given to us on the condition that it be used for the common good of the church.

> As each has received a gift, use it to serve one another, as good stewards of God's varied grace.
>
> 1 PETER 4:10

The proper use, then, of all the good gifts we have received is the free and generous sharing of those gifts with others. No more certain principle nor more effective exhortation for keeping that rule is imaginable than this: Scripture teaches us that all the gifts we utilize are given to us by God. And they are given along with this law of our faith—that they be put to use for the good of our neighbors. But Scripture goes even further than this when it compares us and the gifts we've been given to the members of a human body. No member of the body exists to serve itself, nor does each member exist merely for its own private use. Rather, it puts its abilities to use for the other members of the body. Nor does any member of the body alone receive any advantage from itself outside of that which belongs to the entire body. Whatever, therefore, a godly man is able to do, he should do it for his brothers. He should consider his own interests only insofar as he sets his mind on the general edification of the whole church. Let this, then, be our rule for kindness and benevolence: We are merely stewards of whatever gifts God has given to us in order to help our neighbors. We must give an account of our stewardship, and right stewardship is that which is fueled by the rule of love. Consequently, we must not merely join zeal for the good of others with concern for our own well-being, but we must submit concern for our own well-being to the good of others.

To help us better understand that this law of stewardship rightly applies to whatever gifts we receive from Him, God applied this law to the smallest gifts of His kindness in former times. For He commanded that the firstfruits of His people's produce be offered to Him.

The best of the firstfruits of your ground you shall bring into the house of the Lord your God.

EXODUS 23:19

In this way, God's people of old testified that it was wrong to secure any profit from their produce before it was consecrated to God. Now, if God's gifts to us are ultimately sanctified to us after our hands have offered them back to their very author, any use of those gifts that is not perfumed by such an offering will be a corrupt abuse of them. But we would strive in vain to increase the Lord's wealth by offering our gifts to Him. Since, therefore, our kindness—as the Prophet says—cannot reach Him, we should practice it toward His saints who are on earth (Ps. 16:2–3). Thus our charitable gifts are compared to holy sacrifices, since they correspond to those sacrifices that were required by the law (Heb. 13:16). ♦

FURTHERMORE, SO THAT we don't grow weary in doing good (which otherwise would be certain to happen immediately), we must understand the next point put forward by the Apostle—that "love is patient" and "is not irritable." The Lord instructs us to do good to all people throughout the entire world, many of whom are unworthy of such good if judged by their own merit. But Scripture comes to our rescue with the best of reasons for doing good to all people. It teaches us not to regard others according to their own merits, but to consider in them the image of God to which we owe both honor and love. But the image of God should be more diligently regarded in those who are of the household of faith, because it has been renewed and restored in them by the Spirit of Christ.

> So then, as we have opportunity, let us do good to everyone, and especially to those who are of the household of faith.
>
> GALATIANS 6:10

Therefore, you have no cause to evade anyone who stands before you and needs your service. Suppose he's a stranger. The Lord, however, has stamped him with His own mark that's familiar to you, and for that reason God forbids you to despise your own flesh. Suppose he is contemptible and worthless. The Lord, however, shows him to be one whom He has condescended to decorate with His own image. Suppose you owe him nothing for what he's done. But God—to whom you know you are obligated because of His many wonderful benefits to you—puts Himself, as it were, in that person's place. Suppose he is unworthy of even your smallest labors for his sake. But the image of God, according to which this person is commended to you, warrants your giving of yourself and your all. Supposing a man not only deserves nothing good from you, but he has also provoked you with injustices and injuries—even this is not just cause for you to stop embracing him with affection and fulfilling your duties of love to him. He has deserved, you might say, something much different from me. But what has the Lord deserved? When He orders you to forgive that man for whatever sin he has committed against you, He calls you to do so not because that man deserves it, but because God Himself has forgiven you (Luke 17:3–4). This is the only path to achieving that which is not only difficult for, but entirely adverse to, our human nature—that is, loving those who hate us, repaying evil with good, and blessing those who curse us.

> But I say to you, Love your enemies and pray for those who persecute you.
>
> MATTHEW 5:44

We must be sure not to dwell on the wickedness of men, but rather to consider the image of God in them. That image, concealing and obliterating their shortcomings, entices us by its beauty and dignity to love and welcome them. ♦

THIS SELF-MORTIFICATION, THEREFORE, will only take place in us when we fulfill the sum of love's requirements. And we fulfill these requirements not when we merely perform all the external duties of love—even if we don't overlook any of them—but when we do so from a sincere affection of love. For it might happen that someone fully performs his obligations as external duties go, and yet he is far from performing them for the right reason. For example, you may see certain people who want to appear very generous, and yet they give nothing without resenting the recipients of their generosity by their proud expressions or arrogant words. Hence the wretchedness into which this unhappy age has sunk—that hardly any charitable gifts are given, at least by the majority of men, without contempt for those to whom they are given. Such viciousness would not have been tolerated even among the pagans of old.

Something more is required from Christians than wearing a cheerful face and rendering their duties attractive by friendly words. First, they should imagine themselves in the situation of that person who needs their help, and they should pity his bad fortune as if they themselves both bore it and felt it. Thus they will be compelled, by a feeling of mercy and humanity, to give him help as if it were given to themselves. One who has this mind-set and approaches the task of helping his brothers will not contaminate his duties to others with arrogance or resentment. He won't despise a brother whom he helps because his brother needs such help, nor will he subject his brother to himself as a debtor. We would of course never mock an injured limb which the rest of the body labors to revive, nor would we consider that limb particularly indebted to the body's other members because it has received more help than it has given. The help that different members of the body mutually offer one another should not—according to the law of nature—be considered a favor, but rather as an obligation that would be unnatural to refuse. For this same reason, one who has performed a single obligation should not consider himself free from doing more—as generally happens when a wealthy person, after offering something of his own, leaves it to others to see to remaining needs, as if such remaining needs had nothing to do with him.

Rather, everyone should consider himself—however great he may be—a debtor to his neighbors. And he must set no limit to the exercise of kindnesses toward others short of the failure of his own resources. For such kindnesses, as far and as wide as they extend, should conform to the rule of love. ♦

LET'S DISCUSS AGAIN more fully the chief part of our self-denial, which, as I've said, relates to God. I've mentioned many things about this that would be superfluous to repeat.[3] It will suffice here to discuss how self-denial forms us to be calm and patient in this life.

First of all, then, in striving for either convenience or tranquility in this present life, Scripture calls us to resign our wills and everything that is

---

3 For example, in Calvin's discussion of repentance and mortification of sin (*Institutes* 3.3.2–3).

ours to the Lord, and to turn the affections of our hearts over to Him to be tamed and bridled.

> Your kingdom come, your will be done, on earth as it is in heaven.
>
> MATTHEW 6:10

Our lust is furious and our greed limitless in pursuing wealth and honors, chasing after power, heaping up riches, and gathering all those vain things which seem to give us grandeur and glory. On the other hand, we greatly fear and hate poverty, obscurity, and humility, and so we avoid these realities in every way. Thus, we see that those who order their lives according to their own counsel have a restless disposition. We see how many tricks they try, how many pursuits they exhaust themselves with in order to secure the objects of their ambition or greed, while trying to avoid, on the other hand, poverty and humility.

Therefore, in order not to be entangled in such snares, godly men must hold this course: First of all, they must neither desire, nor aspire, nor expect to prosper for any other reason than the Lord's blessing. Therefore, let them safely and confidently cast themselves on and rest in that blessing. The flesh might seem beautifully sufficient to itself while it strives by its own power, or ascends by its own zeal, or is assisted by the favor of men toward honors and wealth. However, it's nevertheless certain that all these things will come to nothing and that we will accomplish nothing by our talents or efforts, except insofar as the Lord prospers both. But, on the contrary, His blessing by itself finds a way, in spite of every obstacle, to bring all things to a glad and prosperous end for us. Second, we are admittedly able to secure for ourselves, entirely apart from His blessing, something of glory and riches, just as we often see great honors and wealth piled up by ungodly men. Yet whatever we obtain will turn to evil without His blessing, since those on whom God's curse remains do not taste even the smallest amount of true happiness. We obviously shouldn't desire what makes us more miserable. ♦

SUPPOSING WE ACCEPT that the method of obtaining every prosperous and desirable success rests entirely with God's blessing, and that without God's blessing, every kind of misery and misfortune awaits us. It then also stands that we should not greedily strive for wealth and honors, whether trusting in our own natural skill or persistence, relying on the favor of men, or resting on a hollow dream of good fortune. On the contrary, we should always look to the Lord, that by His care we might be led to whatever lot in life He provides for us.

The result of this will be, in the first place, that we won't rush forward to capture wealth and lay hold of honors through unlawful acts and treachery, evil devices, or greed, to the injury of our neighbors.

Rather, we will follow after those things that don't draw us away from innocence. For who can continue to hope for the help of divine blessing while committing various evils, theft, and other wickedness? For just as God's blessing doesn't come to anyone except those who are pure in thought and deed, so also does that blessing call back from impure thoughts and perverse actions all those who seek it.

Second, a bridle will be placed on us so that we won't burn with untamed lust for growing rich or greedily desiring honors. Isn't it shameful for one to look for God's help to obtain those things which he desires when those things are contrary to God's Word? For that which God curses with His own mouth He will not accompany with the help of His blessing.

Finally, if our hope and desire don't succeed, we will nevertheless be restrained from being impatient and cursing our condition, whatever it may be. For we will understand that such cursing of our condition would be murmuring against God who distributes riches, poverty, honor, and contempt according to His will. In summary, the one who rests on God's blessing in the manner that I've described won't employ wicked means—he knows he'll gain nothing—in the frantic pursuit of things men typically pursue. If he prospers, he won't attribute this to himself or to his own diligence, industry, or luck. Rather, he will acknowledge God as the author of his good fortune.

A person cannot receive even one thing unless it is given him from heaven.

JOHN 3:27

If the affairs of others prosper while he makes little progress, or even regresses, he will endure his poverty with greater patience and moderation of spirit than an impious man would endure minor success that does not precisely meet his desire. For he has this comfort, which provides greater security to him than the highest peak of wealth or power—he knows that his affairs are ordered by the Lord and, as such, promote his salvation. We see this sentiment in David, who, while following God and entrusting himself to God's rule, declared: "I do not occupy myself with things too great and marvelous for me. But I have calmed and quieted my soul, like a weaned child with its mother" (Ps. 131:1–2). ♦

THERE ARE OTHER circumstances in which those who are pious should stand firm in peace and patience. Such qualities should extend to every situation that we encounter in this life. No one, then, has properly denied himself except the one who has entirely abandoned himself to the Lord so that every aspect of his life will be governed by His will. The person thus composed in soul will neither judge himself to be miserable, nor will he spitefully complain against God for his lot in life, come what may.

The true necessity of having such a disposition is clear if you consider how many unforeseen events we are exposed to in this life. We are continually harassed by one illness or another: the plague advances; we are cruelly vexed by the calamities of war; frost and hail render the land barren and leave us with little, devouring our expectation for the year's crop. Wife, parents, children, and close relatives are snatched away by death; homes are consumed by fire. These are events which make men curse their lives, despise the day they were born, hold in contempt heaven and its light, rage against God, and, being fluent in blasphemies, accuse God of unfairness and cruelty. But the believer must in these same circumstances consider the mercy and the fatherly kindness of God. If the believer, then, should see his house made lonely by the loss of those nearest to him, even then he must not stop praising the Lord. Rather, he must turn himself to this thought: "The Lord's grace continues to dwell in my home and will not leave it desolate." If the believer should see his crop consumed by drought, disease, or frost, or trampled down by hail and famine threaten him, even then he must not despair within his soul, nor should he become angry toward God. Rather, he must persist with confidence in this truth: "But we your people, the sheep of your pasture, will give thanks to you forever" (Ps. 79:13). God, then, will provide for us, however barren the land. If the believer should be afflicted by illness, he must not be so stung by the severity of his hardship that he erupts in impatience and demands from God an explanation. Rather, he must, considering the justice and gentleness of God's discipline, recall himself to patience.

Indeed, the believer should accept whatever comes with a gentle and thankful heart, because he knows that it is ordained by the Lord. Moreover, he must not stubbornly resist the rule of God into whose power he has placed himself and all his affairs. So let the Christian make it his priority to drive from his breast that foolish and unfortunate comfort of pagans, who, in order to bolster their spirits against all adverse events, credit those events to fortune. They think it's silly to be angry at fortune, since she is reckless, aimless, and blind—inflicting her wounds equally on the deserving and the undeserving. In contrast, the rule of godliness is to recognize that God's hand is the sole judge and governor of every fortune, and because His hand is not recklessly driven to fury, it distributes to us both good and ill according to His orderly righteousness.

CHAPTER

BEARING OUR CROSS

IS A PART OF SELF-DENIAL

THE GODLY MIND, however, must rise even higher—that is, to that place that Christ calls His disciples when He bids every one of them to take up his cross.

> Then Jesus told his disciples, "If anyone would come after me, let him deny himself and take up his cross and follow me."
>
> MATTHEW 16:24

For those whom the Lord has chosen and condescended to welcome into fellowship with Him should prepare themselves for a life that is hard, laborious, troubled, and full of many and various kinds of evil. For it's the will of their heavenly Father to test them in this way so that He might prove them by trials. Having begun this way with Christ, His only-begotten Son, He continues similarly with all His children.

For although Christ is the Son, beloved before all others—the one in whom the Father's soul delights—we nevertheless see how little ease and comfort Christ experienced (Matt. 3:17; 17:5). Indeed, it could be said that He not only had a cross continually placed upon Him when He lived on earth, but even that His life was nothing other than a kind of perpetual cross. Scripture gives the reason for this: It was necessary that Christ "learned obedience through what he suffered" (Heb. 5:8). Why, then, would we exempt ourselves from the same situation to which Christ our head was subjected—particularly since He was subjected to suffering for our sake to provide for us a pattern of patience in Himself? On this account the Apostle Paul teaches that all God's children are appointed to this end—to be made like Christ.

> For those whom he foreknew he also predestined to be conformed to the image of his Son, in order that he might be the firstborn among many brothers.
>
> **ROMANS 8:29**

From this also we receive remarkable consolation, that in the midst of dark and difficult circumstances, which we consider hostile and evil, we share in Christ's sufferings. For just as He entered into heavenly glory from a labyrinth involving every kind of evil, so we, in the same way, are led through various trials. And thus Paul himself says in another place that as long as we are learning to share in His suffering, we will know the power of His resurrection (Phil. 3:10). If it has been allotted us to share in His death, then we are prepared to share in the glory of His resurrection. How perfectly suited this reality is to lessening the severity of every cross—the more we are afflicted with adverse circumstances, so much more certainly is our communion with Christ confirmed. By virtue of this communion, sufferings themselves not only become blessings to us, but they also serve to promote our salvation. ♦

MOREOVER, OUR LORD in no way had to take upon Himself the bearing of a cross except to prove and testify to His own obedience to His Father. However, there are many reasons why we ourselves must spend our lives subject to a constant cross. First of all, there's the fact that unless our own weaknesses are regularly displayed to us, we easily overestimate our own virtue, being by nature inclined to attribute all good things to our own doing. We don't doubt that our virtue will remain whole and unconquered in the face of whatever difficulties may come. Thus, we're drawn into a foolish and inflated view of our flesh. And then, trusting in our flesh, we brazenly exalt ourselves before God Himself, acting as if our own abilities are sufficient without His grace. There's no better method for God to curb such arrogance than by demonstrating to us through experience our weakness and frailty. He afflicts us with disgrace, poverty, childlessness, illness, and other troubles. And we, for our part, quickly crumble before such blows, being far from able to withstand them. Thus humbled, we learn to call on His strength, which alone can make us stand under the weight of such affliction. Indeed, the holiest among us know they stand by God's grace and not by their own virtues. Yet they would nevertheless become too confident in their own courage and constancy if they weren't led to a more intimate knowledge of themselves by the testing of the cross.

Such sluggish self-confidence even snuck up on David: "As for me, I said in my prosperity, 'I shall never be moved.' By your favor, O Lord, you made my mountain stand strong; you hid your face; I was dismayed" (Ps. 30:6–7). Thus David admits that when his affairs prospered, his sensibilities were confounded, so that he neglected the grace of God on which he should have relied and trusted rather than in himself. He assured himself of his own permanence. If this happened to so great a prophet as David, each of us should tremble and take caution. While men, then, delude themselves during times of tranquility with a notion of their own great constancy and patience, they learn the truth about themselves when humbled by times of difficulty. Believers, being warned of their own weaknesses by such proofs, make progress toward humility and, shedding their perverse confidence in their flesh, cast themselves on the grace of God. When they have so cast themselves on the grace of God, they experience the presence of divine power in which there is sufficient and abundant help. ♦

MOREOVER, PAUL TEACHES that "suffering produces endurance, and endurance produces character" (Rom. 5:3–4). For God has promised believers that He will be with them in times of suffering. Believers, being upheld by God's hand, experience this truth while they patiently endure such times. For they're unable to endure such suffering in their own strength. Therefore, as saints endure suffering, they experience

God's providing of the strength He has promised to give in times of need. And so their hope is also made strong. It would be ungrateful for them not to expect that they'll discover—in the end—how constant and sure God's truth is.

We see now how many related benefits are born from the cross. The cross destroys the false notion of our own strength that we've dared to entertain, and it destroys that hypocrisy in which we have taken refuge and pleasure. It strips us of carnal self-confidence, and thus humbling us, instructs us to cast ourselves on God alone so that we won't be crushed or defeated. Such victory is followed by hope, since the Lord—by providing what He has promised—establishes His truthfulness for what lies ahead. Even for these reasons alone, it's clear how vital the discipline of the cross is for us. It's no little thing to be stripped of our blind self-love and thus to be made aware of our own weakness. Moreover, having been impressed with our own weakness, we learn to despair of ourselves. Then, having despaired of ourselves, we transfer our trust to God. Next, we rest in our trust in God, and we rely on His help and persevere unconquered to the end. Then standing on His grace, we see that He is true to His promises. Finally, being confident in the certainty of His promises, our hope is strengthened. ♦

ANOTHER REASON THE Lord afflicts His people is to test their endurance and to train them in obedience. They are quite unable to produce obedience unless He Himself empowers them. But it pleases Him to illuminate and testify by clear proofs to those graces that He has bestowed on the saints, so that those graces don't lie hidden and idle. In Scripture, therefore, God is said to test His servants' endurance when He puts on display that strength and constancy in suffering that He has given to them.

So God tested Abraham and verified his piety

when Abraham didn't refuse to sacrifice his one and only son.

> But the angel of the Lord called to him from heaven and said, "Abraham, Abraham!" And he said, "Here I am." He said, "Do not lay your hand on the boy or do anything to him, for now I know that you fear God, seeing you have not withheld your son, your only son, from me."
>
> GENESIS 22:11–12

Peter likewise teaches that our faith is proven by trials, just as gold is refined in a furnace of fire. Shouldn't this most excellent gift of endurance, which believers receive from their God, be put to use and made certain and evident? Otherwise, men would never value the gift of endurance according to its true worth. But God Himself acts justly when He ordains circumstances that excite the virtues He has given to believers, so that those virtues don't escape notice or, indeed, remain unused and waste away. There is, then, good reason for difficult circumstances in the lives of the saints, since they create endurance in them.

Believers are also trained in obedience by means of the cross. For thus they are taught to live according to God's will rather than their own. If everything went according to their own plans, they would never know what it means to follow God. Even the philosopher Seneca refers to an old proverb in which individuals were told to "follow God" when being encouraged to endure adversity.[1] This proverb hinted at the truth that a person truly and finally submits to God's yoke when his hand and his back are exposed to God's discipline. Therefore, we shouldn't run from all the ways in which our heavenly Father shapes us in obedience, for it's right that we prove ourselves obedient to Him in every circumstance. ♦

---

1   Seneca expresses this sentiment in his work *On the Happy Life*.

BUT IF WE want to grasp how much we need such training in obedience, we must recall how prone our flesh is to cast off God's yoke as soon as it enjoys any period of relative peace and quiet. Our flesh is like a stubborn horse that becomes wild and unmanageable and doesn't recognize its rider—however much it previously obeyed his commands—after several days spent idly grazing. We continually find in ourselves that which God lamented in the people of Israel. Growing fat and lazy, we buck against Him who has fed and nourished us.

> But Jeshurun grew fat, and kicked;
>   you grew fat, stout, and sleek;
> then he forsook God who made him
>   and scoffed at the Rock of his salvation.
>
> **DEUTERONOMY 32:15**

God's kindness should cause us to reflect on and delight in His goodness. But our perverse ingratitude is such that we make His kindness a means of growing ever more spoiled. Thus, we must be restrained by some discipline so that we don't break forth in obstinacy—acting wickedly because of our great wealth, becoming puffed up with pride because of honors, or growing arrogant because we possess other goods in ourselves or our circumstances. The Lord Himself providentially opposes, conquers, and restrains the ferocity of our flesh by the medicine of the cross. He does this in ways that uniquely serve each believer's well-being. For we're not all equally or severely oppressed by the same diseases. Nor do we all require the same exact cure. And so we see that each believer is subjected to a different kind of cross. Our heavenly doctor, having purposed to restore all of us to health, treats some more leniently. Meanwhile, He applies stronger remedies to others. But none of us is left untouched by or remains immune to His medicine—He knows we are all diseased. ♦

MOREOVER, IN ORDER to keep us in proper obedience to Himself, our merciful Father not only anticipates our weaknesses but also regularly corrects our past failings. Thus, when we are afflicted, we should immediately call to mind our past life. As we do so, we will undoubtedly discover that our past failings are worthy of whatever discipline we receive.

Nevertheless, we shouldn't let awareness of our past sins serve as the principal reason for the call to endure suffering. Scripture supplies a more profound reason for us when it teaches that in adverse circumstances we're being disciplined by the Lord so that we won't be condemned with the world.

> But when we are judged by the Lord, we are disciplined so that we may not be condemned along with the world.
>
> 1 CORINTHIANS 11:32

Therefore, in the midst of the bitterness of tribulations, we should recognize the kindness and mercy of our Father toward us. For even in such tribulations, He doesn't cease to promote our salvation. Indeed, He afflicts us not to ruin or destroy us, but instead to deliver us from the condemnation of the world. This awareness leads us to what Scripture teaches in another place: "My son, do not despise the Lord's discipline or be weary of his reproof, for the Lord reproves him whom he loves, as a father the son in whom he delights" (Prov. 3:11–12). When we discern our Father's rod of discipline in our lives, shouldn't we present ourselves to Him as obedient and teachable sons rather than as obstinate and hopeless men who've become hardened in wrongdoing?

If God didn't call us back to Himself by means of correction when we fell from Him, He would destroy us. Thus, it's rightly said in Scripture that we are illegitimate children, not sons, if we are without discipline.

If you are left without discipline, in which all have participated, then you are illegitimate children and not sons.

HEBREWS 12:8

Therefore, we are indeed wicked if we shun Him while He manifests to us His kindness and His care for our salvation. Scripture teaches that there's a difference between believers and unbelievers. Unbelievers become worse and more obstinate in consequence of the lashes they receive, just like slaves of earnest and deep-seated wickedness. Believers repent just like individuals gifted with the status of sonship. Choose, then, which of these you will be. But since I have spoken elsewhere on this subject,[2] I will end this discussion, satisfied to have briefly touched on it here. ♦

---

2   See Calvin's discussion of repentance, rebirth, and indwelling sin (*Institutes* 3.3.9–11).

FURTHERMORE, WE HAVE a particular consolation when we suffer persecution for righteousness' sake. In such persecution, we should consider how much God, thus branding us with the mark that His soldiers bear, condescends to honor us. When I speak of suffering for righteousness' sake, I have in mind not just those who are oppressed for their defense of the gospel, but also those who encounter oppression for whatever ways they defend righteousness. Whether, then, we assert God's truth against Satan's lies or take up the cause of the good and innocent against the injustices of the wicked, we will necessarily encounter the world's displeasure and hatred. And from that may follow danger to our lives, our property, and our honor. In these circumstances, we shouldn't think it painful or troublesome to devote ourselves to God in such a way. We shouldn't judge ourselves miserable, when by His own mouth He has pronounced us blessed.

Blessed are those who are persecuted
for righteousness' sake, for theirs is the
kingdom of heaven.

MATTHEW 5:10

Poverty is in fact misery if we consider it in and of itself. Exile, scorn, imprisonment, and dishonor are likewise misery. And then there's death, the final calamity. But when God's favor rests on us, none of these things need threaten our happiness. Let us therefore derive greater contentment from Christ's testimony about us than from the vain estimations of our own flesh.

Thus it will be that, following the example of the Apostles, we will rejoice when He considers us worthy to suffer disgrace for His name (Acts 5:41). What then? Though innocent and clear of conscience, we might be stripped of our resources by the wickedness of the ungodly, and so reduced to poverty in the view of men—but before God in heaven our riches are thereby truly increased. We might be thrust out of our homes, but thereby we are drawn more intimately into God's household. We might be harassed and despised, but thereby we drive deeper roots into Christ. We might be branded with disgrace and dishonor, but thereby we gain a more honorable rank in the kingdom of God. We might be slaughtered, but thereby a door unto the blessed life is opened to us. We ought to be ashamed to think less of those things on which God places such value than we do of this present life's shadowy and fleeting pleasures. ♦

SCRIPTURE, THEN, ABUNDANTLY comforts us by these and similar teachings when we experience dishonor and harm for our defense of what's right. Thus, we show ourselves ungrateful if we don't freely and gladly receive such dishonor and harm from the hand of the Lord. This form of the cross, by which Christ wills to be glorified in us, is unique to believers—just as Peter also teaches.

> If you are insulted for the name of Christ, you are blessed, because the Spirit of glory and of God rests upon you.
>
> **1 PETER 4:14**

But since we, by natural impulse, judge dishonorable treatment worse than a hundred deaths, Paul reminds us that as Christians we will experience not only persecution but also disgrace. This is because we hope in the living God (1 Tim. 4:10). Elsewhere, Paul bids us to walk after his own example, whether people slander us or praise us (2 Cor. 6:8).

But the gladness that is required from us in the midst of persecution doesn't destroy every feeling of anguish and sorrow. For the saints' endurance regarding the cross wouldn't be called endurance if they weren't tormented with sorrow and choked with grief. If there were no difficulty in poverty, no suffering in illness, no sting in disgrace, no horror in death, then we would face these things indifferently—and what courage or perseverance could then be credited to us? Each of these things, by virtue of their own inherent bitterness, might naturally and entirely consume our souls. But in the midst of them, the courage of the believer makes itself known. Though severely oppressed and touched by the feeling of some bitterness, the believer, nevertheless, courageously fights that feeling and in the end perseveres. In the midst of these feelings, the endurance of the believer reveals itself. Though mercilessly provoked, the believer is nevertheless restrained by the fear of God from bursting forth in anger. In the midst of them, the steadfastness of the believer shines. Though wounded by sorrow and grief, he finds rest in the spiritual comfort of his God. ♦

PAUL FITTINGLY DESCRIBES the war that believers wage against natural feelings of anguish in their pursuit of endurance and perseverance: "We are afflicted in every way, but not crushed; perplexed, but not driven to despair; persecuted, but not forsaken; struck down, but not destroyed" (2 Cor. 4:8–9). We see that bearing the cross with endurance doesn't mean that a person is absolutely stupefied or robbed of every feeling of sorrow. The Stoics of old foolishly idealized such a person—one who, having stripped himself of all humanity, feels the same whether he encounters adversity or prosperity, sorrow or success; or rather one who feels nothing—like a stone. And what did the Stoics achieve by such sublime wisdom? They painted a portrait of endurance that has never been found, nor can exist, among men. Indeed, while they wished to represent endurance accurately and precisely, they deprived humankind of the power of genuine endurance.

At present, likewise, there are among Christians new Stoics who think it a vice not only to groan and weep, but even to be sad or upset. And indeed, these ridiculous ideas generally come from idle men. They employ themselves more in observation than in action, and they can produce nothing more than fantasies. But this cruel philosophy is nothing to us. Our Master and Lord condemned it not only by word but also by example. Our Lord groaned and wept, both for His own and others' difficult circumstances. Nor did He teach His disciples anything different: "The world," He said, "will rejoice, but you will weep and lament" (John 16:20). And, so that no one should turn such weeping and lamenting into sin, He expressly declared those who mourn to be blessed.

> Blessed are those who mourn, for they shall be comforted.
>
> MATTHEW 5:4

And no wonder. For if all tears are condemned, what will we make of our very own Lord, from whose body trickled tears of blood (Matt. 26:28; Luke 22:44)? If all fear is judged faithlessness, what place will we give to that dread which according to Scripture heavily oppressed Him? If all sadness should be dismissed, how will we accept that His soul was sorrowful even unto death (Matt. 26:38)? ♦

I'VE SAID THESE things about our experience of grief in order to keep godly people from despair—to keep them, that is, from immediately abandoning the pursuit of endurance because they cannot rid themselves of a natural feeling of sorrow. Such despair and abandonment will come to those who turn endurance into indifference. They will turn a courageous and faithful man into a wooden post. Rather, Scripture praises the saints for endurance when we, though knocked around by evil circumstances, remain unbroken and undefeated; when we, though pricked by bitterness, are simultaneously filled with spiritual joy; when we, though oppressed by anxiety, breathe freely—cheered by the consolation of God. Nevertheless, there lives within our hearts a revulsion to evil circumstances because of our natural disposition, which flees and shrinks back from adverse realities. Yet godly affection strives after obedience to the divine will, even in the midst of such difficulties. Such revulsion to adversity was noted by our Lord when He said to Peter: "When you were young, you used to dress yourself and walk wherever you wanted, but when you are old, you will stretch out your hands, and another will dress you and carry you where you do not want to go" (John 21:18).

It is, of course, unlikely that Peter, when it came time for him to glorify God through his death, was dragged to it unwilling and resistant. If such had been the case, he would have received little praise for his martyrdom. But even if he obeyed the divine command with the highest degree of enthusiasm in his heart, he was still torn by a divided will, because he couldn't cast off his humanity. When he reflected on the savage death that he would suffer, he was struck with horror, and would have willingly run away. But the thought that he was called to that death by God's own command then came to his aid, conquering and trampling his fear, so that he willingly and cheerfully submitted himself to death.

If, then, we want to be disciples of Christ, we should make it our aim to soak our minds in the sort of sensitivity and obedience to God that can tame and subdue every natural impulse contrary to His command. So it will be that no matter what kind of cross is placed upon us, we will steadily maintain endurance even through the narrowest straits of the soul. Indeed, adverse circumstances will keep their bitterness, and we will feel their bite. When afflicted by illness, we will groan and toss and long for health. When pursued by poverty, we will feel the stings of sadness and anxiety. We will bear the weight of sorrow at dishonor, contempt, and injustice. When loved ones die, we will naturally weep. But this will always be our conclusion: Nevertheless, the Lord has willed it. Therefore, let us follow His will. Indeed, this thought must intervene in the midst of sorrow's very stings, in the midst of our groans and tears, in order to incline our hearts to endure those things with which they're inflicted. ♦

SINCE WE HAVE found in God's will the main reason to endure the cross, I should briefly explain the difference between a Christian approach to suffering and one promoted by the worldly wisdom of the philosophers. In truth, very few philosophers have attained the height of realizing that God's hand forms us through affliction, or who have recognized that our role in affliction is to submit to God. Indeed, they offer no reason for enduring suffering except that such suffering is a fact of life. But this is nothing other than to say, "We must submit to God, since it is vain to struggle against Him." If, however, we submit to God only because we judge suffering necessary—supposing we could escape—then we no longer genuinely obey God.

But Scripture bids us to see something much different in God's will—namely, fairness and justice, and then concern for our salvation.

> And we know that for those who love
> God all things work together for good,
> for those who are called according to his
> purpose.
>
> ROMANS 8:28

And thus Christian exhortations to endure suffering are of this sort: Whether we suffer poverty, exile, imprisonment, contempt, sickness, childlessness, or any such thing, let us remember that nothing happens apart from God's pleasure and providence, and that God Himself does nothing that isn't perfectly in order. What then? Don't our innumerable and frequent faults deserve more severe and weighty punishments than those that He, according to His mercy, has placed on us? Isn't it fair that our flesh be tamed and made familiar with the yoke in order to keep it from running wild with lust according to its natural disposition? Are God's justice and truth not worthy causes to suffer for?

But if God's impartiality is truly made apparent in our sufferings, we cannot complain or struggle against them without fault. Thus, we don't hear that frigid song: "Yield, for such suffering is necessary." We hear, rather, instruction that is lively and full of power: "Submit, because it is not right to resist. Endure, because unwillingness to do so is defiance of God's justice." But since in the end we only find attractive those things that we perceive to be for our good and well-being, our kind Father comforts us also in this way—assuring us that He works for our salvation by that very cross with which He afflicts us. If it's clear that tribulations work toward our salvation, shouldn't we accept them with a grateful and calm spirit? In bearing them with endurance, we're not yielding to necessity, but we're assenting to our own good.

Such considerations will bear this fruit: However much our spirits might shrink beneath the cross, naturally adverse to its bitterness, they will expand in equal measure with spiritual joy. And this will give rise to thanksgiving, which cannot exist without joy—thanksgiving and praise of our Lord can only spring from a glad and joyful heart. If there's nothing that can stop such thanksgiving and praise in us, then it's clear that the bitterness of the cross must be tempered with spiritual joy.

CHAPTER

MEDITATION ON

OUR FUTURE LIFE

IN WHATEVER TROUBLE comes to us, we should always set our eyes on God's purpose to train us to think little of this present life and inspire us to think more about the future life. For God knows well that we are greatly inclined to love this world by natural instinct. Thus, He uses the best means to draw us back and shake us from our slumber, so that we don't become entirely stuck in the mire of our love for this world.

We all, throughout our entire lives, want to act as though we were longing for heavenly immortality and striving urgently after it. Indeed, we judge it shameful not to distinguish ourselves in some way from the brute animals, whose condition would be much the same as ours if we didn't hope for eternity after death. But examine the plans, pursuits, and actions of whomever you wish, and you'll find them to be entirely earthly. Thus we see our stupidity. Our minds, having been dulled by the blinding glare of empty wealth, power, and honor, can see no farther than these things. And our hearts, burdened with greed, ambition, and lust for gain, can rise no higher than these things. In sum, our entire soul, entangled in the enticements of the flesh, seeks its happiness on earth.

In order to resist this wickedness, the Lord teaches His people about the emptiness of this present life through constant lessons in suffering. Thus, so that His people don't promise themselves lofty and untroubled peace in this life, He often permits them to be troubled and harassed by wars, uprisings, robberies, and other injuries. So that they don't gawk with too much greediness at frail and tottering riches, or rest on those they already possess, He reduces them to poverty—or at least restricts them to very little wealth—through exile, barrenness of land, fire, or other means. So that they aren't enticed too much by the advantages of married life, He lets them be frustrated by the offenses of their spouse, humbles them by the wickedness of their children, or afflicts them with the loss of a child. However, there are times when God deals more gently with His people. Yet even when He does, so that they don't become puffed up with pride or inflated with self-confidence, He sets before their eyes disease and danger to teach them how unstable and fleeting are those good things that come to men, who are subject to death.

It is good for me that I was afflicted,
that I might learn your statutes.

PSALM 119:71

In the end, we rightly profit from the discipline of the cross when we learn that this life, considered in itself, is troubled, turbulent, attended by many miseries, and never entirely happy, and that whatever things we consider good in this life are uncertain, passing, vain, and spoiled because they're mixed with many evils. And from this we likewise conclude that we should expect and hope for nothing other than trouble in this life, and that we should set our eyes on heaven where we expect our crown. So, indeed, we ought to realize that our souls will never seriously rise to the desire and contemplation of the future life until they've been soaked in scorn for this present life. ♦

THERE'S NO MIDDLE ground between these two things: either earth must become worthless to us, or we must remain bound by the chains of extravagant love for it. If, then, we care for eternity, we must make every effort to free ourselves from those chains. Of course, this present life has many attractions that entice us—many displays of comfort, charm, and sweetness. So that we are not enchanted, we must be continually pulled away from such temptations. What would become of us if we enjoyed perpetual good fortune and delight, since even regular stings of misfortune fail to awaken us to proper reflection on our misery? Man's life is like a vapor or shadow.

> What is your life? For you are a mist that appears for a little time and then vanishes.
>
> JAMES 4:14

Not only the learned understand this. Ordinary people also know this well-worn truth, and—judging it useful to remember—have highlighted it in many famous proverbs. But there's nothing we bring to mind and think about less diligently than this truth. For we all make our plans as if we were constructing immortality for ourselves in this world. If we pass by a funeral or walk among graves, then—because our eyes are confronted with the image of death—we eloquently philosophize on the emptiness of life. But even this doesn't always happen, for these things often don't make an impression on us. And even when they do, our love of wisdom is momentary. It vanishes as soon as we turn our backs and leaves without a trace in our memory. In short, it fades like the applause in the theater of some pleasant show. Forgetting not just death, but even mortality itself—as if no rumor of it had ever reached our ears—we return to the lazy security of earthly immortality. If, in the meantime, someone interrupts us with the proverb that man is but a momentary thing, we admit this to be so, but give so little attention to it that the notion of our permanence remains firmly impressed on our minds.

Who, therefore, can deny how valuable it is not only to be reminded about the miserable condition of our earthly life with words, but to be convinced of it by things that happen to us? This is especially so since, even when overcome by life's miseries, we barely manage to stop staring at this present life with depraved and stupid admiration, as if it contained within itself the sum of our greatest goods. But if God desires to teach us in this way, it's our duty in turn to hear Him when He calls to us, waking us from our slumber so that we might strive with our whole heart toward contempt of the world and meditation on the future life. ♦

HOWEVER, THE CONTEMPT for this present life that believers should cultivate shouldn't produce hatred of this life or ingratitude toward God. This life, though bursting at the seams with every kind of misery, should still be considered one of God's blessings that shouldn't be dismissed. We're guilty of ingratitude to God if we fail to recognize something of divine blessing in this life. Indeed, believers in particular should see evidence of divine kindness in this life, since everything in it has been designed to further their own salvation. Before He openly presents to us our inheritance of eternal glory, God desires to declare Himself our Father through smaller proofs. Such proofs are the good gifts He daily bestows on us.

If then this life helps us understand God's goodness, should we turn up our noses at it as if it didn't contain even a crumb of advantage to us? Therefore, it's right that we clothe ourselves in this attitude and affection—that we place this life among those gifts of divine kindness that shouldn't be disdained.

Indeed, as if the testimonies of Scripture (which are numerous and clear) were lacking, nature itself also encourages us to return thanks to the Lord. He has brought us into this world's light and He has permitted us to enjoy it. He has lavished on us every necessary mean for life's preservation. And there's much greater reason for gratitude if we remember, while in this life, that we're in some manner being prepared for the glory of His heavenly kingdom. For the Lord has so ordered things that those who will one day be crowned in heaven will first encounter struggles on earth. And so none will triumph until they've survived the difficulties of war and have obtained the victory.

There is, in the next place, another reason for gratitude: We begin in this life, by various blessings, to taste the sweetness of God's kindness. Thus, our hope and desire are provoked to pursue the full expression of His kindness. Once we've concluded that this earthly life of ours is a gift of divine mercy—and grateful recollection of this is our obligation—then we rightly stoop to consider this life's miserable condition. And by such consideration we disentangle ourselves from excessive desire for this life, which—as has been said—is our natural inclination. ◆

OUR DESIRE FOR a better life, then, should increase to the degree that we're dragged away from our twisted love of this life. I confess that those who thought it best not to be born, or almost as good to die young, have reasoned well.[1] Because such men lacked the

---

1   Ancient authors such as Theognis, Herodotus, and Cicero express these sentiments.

light of God and true religion, what could they see in this life that's not foul and unfortunate? Nor were they unreasonable who attended the births of their kindred with grief and tears, but their funerals with solemn joy.[2] Such feeling was unprofitable to them because, lacking the proper instruction of faith, they didn't understand how something that's neither blessed nor desirable in itself could result in good for the righteous. And thus in despair they brought their reasoning to an end.

Therefore, the goal of believers—when they assess this mortal life and realize it's nothing in and of itself but misery—should be to direct themselves wholly, briskly, and freely toward contemplation of that future and eternal life. By way of contrast to that future and eternal life, this present life cannot only be safely disregarded but, in view of that life to

---

2 Such an occasion is recorded by Cicero in his quoting from a lost work of Euripides.

come, thoroughly despised and scorned. If heaven is our home, what is earth but our place of exile? If departure from this world is entrance into life, what is this world but a grave? What is continuing in this life but remaining submerged in death? If being liberated from the body means laying hold of real freedom, what is the body but a prison? If the pinnacle of happiness consists in the enjoyment of God's presence, is it not misery to be without it? But until we escape this world, "we are away from the Lord" (2 Cor. 5:6).

Therefore, earthly life, when compared with heavenly life, must certainly and readily be condemned and despised. It should never be hated, except to the extent that it makes us liable to sin— though properly speaking our hatred should be toward sin, not toward life itself. Although we may be so moved with weariness and hatred of this life that we desire its end, we must be prepared to remain in it according to the Lord's will. And so, our weariness won't result in complaining and impatience. For the Lord has stationed us in an outpost, and we must keep guard here until He calls us home. In truth, Paul, being held captive so long in the bonds of the flesh, lamented his condition, and sighed with a burning desire for deliverance.

> Wretched man that I am! Who will deliver me from this body of death?
>
> ROMANS 7:24

Nevertheless, that he might submit himself to God's rule, he declared himself ready for whatever might come (Phil. 1:23–24). He realized his duty to God was to glorify His name, whether by death or life (Rom. 14:8). But it's God's right to decide what best serves His own glory.

If, then, we must live and die to the Lord, let us leave to Him the decision of when our lives will end. But let us do so in such a way that we burn with desire for the end of this life, and let us remain constant in meditation on the next life. Indeed, considering our future immortality, let us scorn this life. Considering the mastery of sin in this life, let us long to give up this life as soon as it should please the Lord. ◆

IT'S REMARKABLE, HOWEVER, that many who brag about being a Christian are possessed by dread rather than longing for death. And so they tremble at the very mention of death, as if it were an ominous and disastrous thing. It is, of course, ordinary that our natural senses should react to the news of our own undoing. But it's entirely inappropriate that Christians should lack within themselves the light of piety that conquers and suppresses fear by a stronger feeling of consolation. If we remember that this unstable, vicious, corruptible, perishable, decaying, and rotten tabernacle of our flesh will be undone in order to be subsequently renewed in constant, perfect, incorruptible, and—in sum—heavenly glory, then faith will compel us to fervently desire that very death which nature dreads. If we remember that through death we are recalled from exile to dwell at home—indeed, our heavenly home—what can this thought produce but comfort?

Some might object: "Every creature longs to be permanent." I admit the same, of course. In fact, I'm arguing that on this basis we should set our eyes on future immortality, where that permanent condition that never appears on earth will prevail. For Paul rightly teaches believers to approach death cheerfully, not desiring to be unclothed but to be clothed (2 Cor. 5:2–4). Even brute animals and lifeless creatures—even trees and stones—being conscious of their present futility, long for the day of the final resurrection when they will be set free from corruption along with the sons of God.

For the creation waits with eager longing
for the revealing of the sons of God.

ROMANS 8:19

Since we are gifted with the light of intelligence, and, what's more, illumined by God's Spirit, shouldn't we raise our minds higher than this decaying earth when troubled about our existence?

But this is neither the time nor the place to argue about such problems as the fear of death. From the outset of this work I professed that I have little desire to get caught up in lengthy discussions about common topics. Those whose souls are fearful of death should read Cyprian's little book on the subject of death.[3] Or perhaps they should be sent to read the philosophers, whose contempt of death would put such fearful souls to shame. Let us, however, remember this truth: No one has

---

3 Cyprian, *On Mortality.*

made much progress in the school of Christ who doesn't look forward joyfully both to his death and the day of his final resurrection. For Paul identifies all believers by this characteristic.

> For the grace of God has appeared, bringing salvation for all people, training us to renounce ungodliness and worldly passions, and to live self-controlled, upright, and godly lives in the present age, waiting for our blessed hope, the appearing of the glory of our great God and Savior Jesus Christ, who gave himself for us to redeem us from all lawlessness and to purify for himself a people for his own possession who are zealous for good works.
>
> TITUS 2:11–14

And Scripture, so often as it sets forth a reason for solid joy, directs us to consider these things.

"Rejoice," says the Lord, "and lift up your heads, for your redemption draws near."[4] Why should that which the Lord intended to powerfully incite us to rejoicing and cheerfulness produce only sadness and dismay? If this is how we feel, how can we still glory in Him as though He were our master? Let us then arrive at a more sensible frame of mind. Even if the blind and stupid desire of our flesh opposes us, let us not hesitate to desire the Lord's coming—not with wishes alone, but with groans and sighs—as the greatest of all events. For He comes as our Redeemer to rescue us from this immense whirlpool of evils and miseries and to lead us to that blessed inheritance of His own life and glory. ✦

THIS IS CERTAIN: the entire body of believers, so long as they live on earth, must be like sheep destined for slaughter. Thus they are conformed to Christ their

---

4   See Luke 21:28.

head (Rom. 8:36). They will be miserable if they don't set their minds on heaven and so rise above all that's in the world—and pierce the facade of present circumstances (1 Cor. 15:19). When they once have raised their heads above this earth, even though they should see the ungodly decked out in wealth and awards, enjoying the utmost tranquility, flaunting every kind of splendor and luxury, and abounding in every kind of pleasure—even if, moreover, they should be wickedly attacked by the ungodly, haughtily insulted by them, exploited by their greed, or harassed by their desires in some other way—even then believers will bear such evils. For they will set their eyes on that day when the Lord will receive His faithful people into the peace of His kingdom, wipe every tear from their eyes, clothe them in garments of glory and gladness, feed them with the indescribable sweetness of His own pleasures, raise them to fellowship in His own lofty heights, and—at last—grant them participation in

His own happiness (Isa. 25:8; Rev. 7:17). But He will cast the wicked, who have flourished on earth, into utter disgrace. He will turn their pleasures into suffering, their laughter and delight into tears and hissing. He will disturb their tranquility with pains of conscience. He will punish their self-indulgence with unquenchable fire. And He will subject them to the godly, whose patience they have exhausted. For, as Paul testifies, it's right for those who are miserable and have been unjustly afflicted to receive rest, and it's right for the wicked who have tormented the godly to receive affliction, when the Lord Jesus is revealed from heaven (2 Thess. 1:6–7). This, surely, is our great consolation. Robbed of this consolation, we must either despair in our soul, or seek comfort—to our own destruction—in the empty comforts of this world. Indeed, even the prophet himself confessed that his feet nearly slipped when he considered for too long the prosperity of the ungodly in the present age. Nor could he steady himself in any other way than by entering into the sanctuary of God and considering anew the end of the godly and the wicked.

> But when I thought how to understand this,
>   it seemed to me a wearisome task,
> until I went into the sanctuary of God;
>   then I discerned their end.

To sum up everything in a word: The cross of Christ finally triumphs in believers' hearts—over the devil, the flesh, sin, and the wicked—when their eyes are turned to the power of the resurrection.

HOW THE PRESENT LIFE AND

ITS COMFORTS SHOULD BE USED

BY MEANS OF such lessons, Scripture also fully teaches us how we should use the good things of this earth rightly. This is a matter that shouldn't be neglected in composing a rule for life. Since we're alive, we should make use of this life's necessary supports. We shouldn't avoid those things which seem to serve our pleasure more than our necessity. Instead, we should hold to some rule so that we can use the things of this world—whether they serve necessity or delight—with a pure conscience.

The Lord prescribes this rule in His Word when He says that this present life is a kind of pilgrimage for His people, wherein they eagerly travel toward the heavenly kingdom. If they are merely passing through this land, then without doubt they should make use of its goods only insofar as they aid rather than hinder their journey. Thus, it's with good reason that Paul urges us to make use of this world just as if we were not using it, and, similarly, to buy possessions as though we were selling them.

This is what I mean, brothers: the appointed time has grown very short. From now on, let those who have wives live as though they had none, and those who mourn as though they were not mourning, and those who rejoice as though they were not rejoicing, and those who buy as though they had no goods, and those who deal with the world as though they had no dealings with it. For the present form of this world is passing away.

1 CORINTHIANS 7:29–31

But since this is truly slippery ground with steep slopes in every direction, we should strive to set our feet where we can stand safely. There have been some men—good and holy in other respects—who saw that self-indulgence and luxury are, because of unbridled desire, perpetually taken too far. These men understood that self-indulgence and luxury needed to be severely curbed. Thus, in order to correct such a difficult problem, they devised a rule to oppose it—permitting men to use bodily goods only insofar as self-indulgence and luxury were necessities to life. Their counsel was certainly pious, but they were too severe in what they demanded from men. For they bound men's consciences more narrowly than the Word of the Lord binds them—a very dangerous thing to do. In fact, they made it necessary to abstain from everything that's not essential to life. Thus, according to them, it's barely permissible to eat and drink anything more than bread and water. Others were even more severe, such as Crates of Thebes, who reportedly cast his riches into the sea because he believed he would be destroyed by them if they were not destroyed.

But many today look for a loophole so they can excuse the excessive desire of the flesh in using external things. Meanwhile, they wish to pave a way for self-indulgence. And so, they take as fact what I won't concede—that freedom in using external things shouldn't be restrained in any measure, and that it should be left to each man's conscience to make use of externalities as he sees fit. I admit, for my part, that consciences neither can nor should be bound by fixed and precise statutes in these matters. But since Scripture gives us general rules for the proper use of external things, we should certainly restrain ourselves according to those rules. ♦

WE WON'T GO wrong in the use of God's gifts as long as we let their use be governed by their author's purpose in creating and designing them for us—for truly He created them for our good, not our ruin. No one, therefore, will hold a truer course than he who carefully considers this purpose of God's gifts. Thus, if we consider the purpose for which He created food, we find He had regard not only for our necessity but also our pleasure and enjoyment. So too with clothes—the purpose was our adornment and honor in addition to our necessity. In the case of herbs, trees, and fruits, He considered the pleasantness of their appearance and charm of their smell in addition to their various uses. If this weren't true, the prophet couldn't list among God's benefits wine, which gladdens the heart of man, and oil, which makes man's face shine.

> You cause the grass to grow for the livestock
>> and plants for man to cultivate,
> that he may bring forth food from the earth
>> and wine to gladden the heart of man,
> oil to make his face shine
>> and bread to strengthen man's heart.
>
> **PSALM 104:14–15**

Nor could Scripture, in order to commend God's generosity, point out everywhere that He has given all such things to men.

Even the natural qualities of things demonstrate how much and how far we can enjoy them. Would the Lord have dressed the flowers with a beauty that runs freely to meet our eyes if it were wrong to be moved by such beauty? Would He have endowed them with so sweet a fragrance that flows freely into our nostrils if it were wrong to be moved by the pleasantness of such fragrance? Isn't the answer obvious? Has God not distinguished colors in such a way as to make some more pleasing than others? Again I ask, isn't the answer obvious? Isn't it clear that He made gold and silver, ivory and marble attractive—rendering them more precious than other metals or stones? In sum, isn't it obvious that He has given us many praiseworthy things, even though they're not necessary? ◆

LET US, THEN, dismiss that inhuman philosophy that only permits us to use created things out of necessity—a philosophy that spitefully deprives us of the lawful enjoyment of divine kindness and by its very nature reduces man to a block of wood, robbed of all his senses. Yet we must no less diligently oppose our fleshly desires that will rush forward without restraint if not kept in check. And, as noted above, we must understand too that there are those who encourage the desires of the flesh, not denying themselves anything under the pretext of liberty.

To start, desire is bridled when we acknowledge that all things given to us are given in order that we might know their author. This leads us to gratitude for His kindness toward us. But how can we be thankful if we drink and indulge in wine so much that we become dazed—unable to perform the duties of piety to which we are called? How can we know God if our flesh, boiling over from overindulgence of our base desires, so infects our minds with its corruption that we cannot discern what's right or honorable? How can there be thankfulness to God for clothing if, on the basis of our fancy and expensive clothes, we both admire ourselves and look down on others? Or if we let elegance and style open a door to sexual immorality? How can there be acknowledgment of God if our minds are enchanted by the splendor of His gifts?

For many people devote their senses to pleasures so much that their minds are buried in them. Many people are so fascinated with marble, gold, and paintings that they're transformed, as it were, into marble, metal, or painted figures. The scent from the kitchen or other sweet odors so paralyzes them that they lose all spiritual sense of smell. And the same thing is seen with the remaining senses. It's evident, then, that in our present circumstances we should considerably curb such freedom that leads to abuse. We should, rather, conform to Paul's rule that we make no provision for the flesh to gratify its desires.

> But put on the Lord Jesus Christ, and make no provision for the flesh, to gratify its desires.
>
> ROMANS 13:14

For if the desires of the flesh are given too much leeway, they will burst forth without limit or restraint. ♦

THERE IS NO more certain or reliable path for us than contempt of this present life and meditation on heavenly immortality. Two principles follow from this, in order that those who use this world might not be affected by it. First, let those who have wives live as though they had none; let those who buy live as though they did not buy (1 Cor. 7:29, 31). Paul teaches this. Let believers learn to bear scarcity with no less calm and patience than they experience abundance—all with moderation. The one who seeks to hold on to the things of this world lightly puts to death his own immoderate appetite for food and drink. He puts to death cowardice, ambition, pride, haughtiness, and dissatisfaction with respect to his table, his buildings, and his clothes. Indeed, he puts to death every care and affection which might lead him astray or hinder his meditation on heavenly life and his zeal for the improvement of his soul.

What Cato said long ago is true: "Luxury produces much care and much carelessness for virtue."[1] There is also an old proverb that states, "Those who are much occupied with concern for the body generally neglect the soul." Therefore, even if the freedom that believers have with respect to external things cannot be subjected to a fixed formula, it should nevertheless be subjected to this rule: Let them indulge themselves very little. Rather, let them—by a perpetual intention of the heart—aim

---

1 This quotation is attributed to Cato in Ammianus Marcellinus' work on Roman history, *Res Gestae*.

to eliminate their stockpiles of superfluous wealth, and to curb extravagance, and to take caution not to turn things given to them for support into obstacles. ♦

AS A SECOND principle, those who have few possessions must learn to endure patiently their humble circumstances, not becoming agitated with excessive longing after things. Those who keep this rule have made much progress in the school of our Lord, but those who haven't give little proof that they are disciples of Christ. Indeed, numerous vices accompany the longing for earthly possessions. Besides, the one who cannot bear poverty is most likely to exhibit the opposite vice in the midst of prosperity. For example, the one who blushes over his cheap clothes will take pride in his expensive ones. The one unsatisfied with his simple meal, fidgeting with desire for something more significant, will abuse better foods by his lack of self-restraint. The one who struggles to endure his humble and ordinary status, growing agitated in spirit, won't be able to restrain his arrogance if he obtains honor. Therefore, let all those who genuinely pursue piety strive to learn, according to the Apostle's example, both to hunger and to be satisfied, to have much and to suffer poverty.

> I know how to be brought low, and I know how to abound. In any and every circumstance, I have learned the secret of facing plenty and hunger, abundance and need.
>
> PHILIPPIANS 4:12

Moreover, Scripture has a third rule by which it regulates our use of earthly things. I said something about it previously when we dealt with the rules of love.[2] Scripture teaches that everything we

---

2 Calvin here refers to his previous discussion in *Institutes* 3.7.5.

own—everything appointed for our benefit—has been given to us by God's kindness, so that all that we own is like a deposit for which we must one day give an account. Therefore, we should manage our possessions as if these words were constantly sounding in our ears: "Turn in the account of your management" (Luke 16:2). At the same time, we should remember who will receive the account we give—namely, one who has commended self-control, soberness, frugality, and modesty just as much as He has condemned luxury, pride, showiness, and vanity; one who has approved no use of possessions but that which is joined with love; one who has already condemned with His own mouth whatever pleasures drag man's heart away from integrity and purity or muddle his thinking. ♦

FINALLY, IT SHOULD be noted that the Lord bids each of us to consider, in all of life's actions, our calling. For He knows how greatly human nature is inclined to restlessness. He knows the fickleness with which it is carried this way and that. He knows the desire and ambition with which it embraces objects opposed to one another. Therefore, so that by our folly and rashness we don't produce mass confusion, He has ordained particular duties to each one in his station in life. And so that no one should overstep his boundaries, He has identified various stations in life as callings. Every individual's rank in life, therefore, is a kind of post assigned to him by the Lord, to keep him from rushing about rashly for the whole of his life. This distinction, which He has applied to our stations in life, is so necessary that all our actions are judged in relation to it. And this judgment of our actions in relation to our calling is often much different than the judgment that human reason or philosophy makes. Philosophers consider no deed more noble than freeing one's country from a tyrant. Yet the ordinary citizen who lays hands on a tyrant is openly condemned by the voice of the heavenly Judge.

However, I don't want to waste time on numerous examples of this point. It's sufficient that we recognize our calling from the Lord to be the principle and foundation of good works in all our affairs. The one who doesn't frame his actions with reference to his calling will never keep the right course in his duties. He will perhaps occasionally do things that are praiseworthy in appearance, but his actions, whatever value they might have before men, will be rejected before God's throne. Nor will there be consistency in his actions in the various spheres of his life.

Consequently, the one who directs himself toward the goal of observing God's calling will have a life well composed. Free from rash impulses, he won't attempt more than his calling warrants. He will understand that he shouldn't overstep his boundaries. He who lives in obscurity will live an ordinary life without complaint, so that he won't be found guilty of deserting his divinely appointed post. Indeed, in the midst of troubles, hardships, annoyances, and other burdens, he will find great relief when he remembers that God is his guide in all these matters. The magistrate will more gladly attend to his duties. The father will more gladly commit himself to his responsibilities. Each person, in whatever his station in life, will endure and overcome troubles, inconveniences, disappointments, and anxieties, convinced that his burden has been placed upon him by God. Great consolation will follow from all of this. For every work performed in obedience to one's calling, no matter how ordinary and common, is radiant—most valuable in the eyes of our Lord.

SCRIPTURE INDEX

ABOUT THE TRANSLATORS

DR. AARON CLAY DENLINGER is dean of logic and rhetoric schools at Arma Dei Academy in Highlands Ranch, Colo. He holds degrees from Colorado Christian University (B.A.), Westminster Seminary California (M.A.), and the University of Aberdeen (Ph.D.) and is author or editor of numerous books, essays, and articles on early modern theology.

DR. BURK PARSONS is senior pastor of Saint Andrew's Chapel in Sanford, Fla., chief publishing officer for Ligonier Ministries, editor of *Tabletalk* magazine, and a Ligonier Ministries teaching fellow. He is author of *Why Do We Have Creeds?* and editor of *John Calvin: A Heart for Devotion, Doctrine, and Doxology* and *Assured by God: Living in the Fullness of God's Grace*.